When Light Shifts

A Memoir in Poems

When Light Shifts

A Memoir in Poems

by

Jennifer L Freed

Jennifer L Freed

Cover design by Shay Culligan
Cover art by Elizabeth C. Freed

ISBN: 978-1-63980-089-6

Kelsay Books
502 South 1040 East, A-119
American Fork, Utah 84003
Kelsaybooks.com

In honor of my parents
In memory of my brother
In gratitude and love for my husband
and daughters

Acknowledgments

I would like to thank the following publications, in which these poems, some in different versions or under different titles, were first published:

Amsterdam Quarterly: "I'll Be the Safety Net, Stretched Taut, Waiting," parts 3 and 4
Atlanta Review: "My Mother in the Hospital, and My Father—"
Atticus Review: "Unfiltered Light"
The Comstock Review: "As Though" and "He Stays"
Naugatuck River Review: "Broken Love Song"
New Verse News: "Taking This In"
The River: "Thrown"
Rust + Moth: "Leaving"
Schuylkill Valley Journal: "What Then"
Subnivean: "My Father's Heart," "Direction," "From Inside Askew," "Mystery II (an answer)," "Rehab Hospital"
West Trestle Review: "Week After Week"
Willawaw Journal: "This Stage"
The Worcester Review: "The Therapist Asks My Mother to Remember"
Zone 3: "Tilt-a-World"
Wising Up Press; the *Goodness* anthology: "Help"

The following eleven poems, some in different forms, were included in a sequence titled "Cerebral Hemorrhage," awarded the 2020 Samuel Washington Allen Prize by the New England Poetry Club, published on-line (Prizewinner's Anthology 2020) at https://nepoetryclub.org:

"Dim Light," "Manners," "I Call My Mother," "The Hospital Social Worker is Available to Discuss Future Plans," "Scattered," "Mystery (A Question)," "She Can't Be Happy," "She Was Happier in Rehab," "Valiant," "Morning (This Thin-Walled Place Where She Can't Feel at Home)," "Nobody Wants This Battle"

Contents

Part IV

Leaving

This visit, I look at the blue
of my mother's eyes as she talks
with my teenage daughters.

She wears my father's frayed button-down, now mottled
with wood stain and paint. Her hair, cut short,
shows the shape of her skull.

She returns to the garage, slides past the table
she's been sanding, and points out two planters—
glazed ceramic, cobalt blue. From a yard sale.
For me. Too heavy for her.

I take in her laugh, its crooked lower teeth.

When I kiss her, I bend lower than I used to. Her skin
smells of warmth and wood, a lingering of Shalimar.

There she is now,
behind the glass of her front door, one hand raised in goodbye,
mouthing *I love you*
as we pull out of the driveway.

I say to my girls, *Look! Isn't she beautiful?*

and the older one says, *I guess,*
and the younger one says, *But why do you keep saying that?*

And I think I don't know
what to say, but my mouth is already answering. My mouth
says, *Because*
I know she's going to leave.

Part I

The Border

She felt dizzy
in her driveway, while bending
to paint an old rocking chair.

She set herself down
but found vomit there, so crawled
toward someplace clean.

The chipmunks raced on round the junipers.
The sun went on bleaching the clapboards.

He found her curled
in the back of the garage,
shivering, slurring her words.

He held her close, didn't know
what to make of the trembling
ground, the strangely shifting light.

Cerebral Hemorrhage

They say she will die
before morning.

We lean toward her breath,
stroke her hair,

and night   becomes dawn   becomes dusk

and she wakes

      opens her mouth,
        not her eyes.

        A word
          we do not hear.

            Her arm rises, fingers strum air.

        She sinks
      into stillness.

Now they say   *If she lives—*

If
she lives, they can't say   who
she will   be.

We sit
beside her silence,
holding her warmth in our palms,
not knowing
how long to hold on
to *goodbye.*

My Father's Heart

a blue-blind spin on a clear blue day
and he's thrown
the world warps
without her

                              (his heart, his heart, his heart)

at its core
and inside his head, the buzzing—
he is skitter and crackle
is brittle   is glass
he can't sleep he can't
eat he can't slow

                              (his heart, his heart, his heart)

his thoughts—
how they rattle
his breath
shallow
his mouth—full of
words he needs someone

                              (his heart, his heart, his heart)

to hold: that crack in the cellar
he's been planning to patch, and
the right way to jiggle the back door latch,
and the dog he had as a kid, named King,
and Mt. Tom, where he took her the night
he proposed,

                              (his heart, his heart, his heart)

and her cup on the table
her tea   half full   and he can't
write things down—
his dim eyes, his gnarled hands—
but he shouldn't   be the only   one
who knows—

                              (his heart, his heart, his heart)

did he tell her enough that he—
can he walk through a week without—

(his heart, his heart, his heart)

he waits
for her to wake

(his heart, his heart, his heart)

he waits
to know whether—

(his heart, his heart, his heart)
(his heart, his heart, his heart)
(his heart, his heart, his heart)

Midnight, My Father at the Computer

He is falling forward
in his chair,

hitting his head
on the screen.

Still, he delays
leaving his desk.

He's used to being alone
in his office, but not

in their bedroom,
in their bed.

Four Days (In the ICU)

On the occasions she wakes,
she is blurry, fuzzy, foggy, dreamy, her smile sweet, her eyes
too heavy to open.

We feel lucky—
    she can speak, she knows who we are,
        her hand strokes our faces so warmly.

We think
we have only to wait.

We understand that her body
won't work as before,
but we think,
when finally
she fully
awakens, she'll be

her.

Dim Light

In the room with the drawn curtains,
she asks why her head
throbs ... like a train ...

You've been hurt
is the farthest her mind can travel.

She lets me feed her
without wondering why,
lets the nurse balance her on a bedpan
without acting shy.

She laughs
when she can't stand without help.
Says her legs must have fallen asleep.

Manners

When the clusters of doctors come making their rounds,
she apologizes that there aren't enough chairs.
She lifts an upturned palm, gestures—*Have you met*
my husband? My daughter?

She lets them ask all their questions, feel her pulse,
shine their lights in her eyes,
then says she's sorry
she can't offer coffee or tea.

When they smile their goodbyes,
she invites them to visit again.

Rehab Hospital

Your mother's brain   She isn't currently   Someone will need to

Please explain to your father   Please have your father   Given
your father's hearing problems   Given your father's   Do you
have Power of Attorney   your mother's medical   your mother's
legal   your mother's wishes in case of   ?

Please provide a copy of   and a copy of   also a copy of
Please discuss with your father   Please explain to your father
Please send   Please sign

Don't bring food from home   Don't leave her alone with her tray
Don't let her drink anything I mean anything without adding
thickener   Make sure you tell all her visitors   can't emphasize
enough   risk of choking   risk of choking   risk of choking
choking   choking

therapy every   re-evaluate every   schedule posted every
update you every

Always stand on her left   She has no idea she's not   See how
she doesn't   We call this *neglect*—she has left side neglect

The nature of her injury   can no longer automatically   how to
stand   how to go   now a conscious sequence of   requires
extreme concentration

The nature of her injury   extreme difficulty concentrating

We encourage families to watch   so you can learn how to   so
you know what to do when

Please don't talk to her while   her need to focus   Your father
doesn't seem to   Please explain to your father

Please don't help her   Please let her   Your father doesn't
Please remind your father

Your mother is doing so well—she brushed her own teeth
Your mother is doing so well—she held her own spoon
Your mother is doing so well—we'll miss her when

Oh no, we don't do that   Rehab hospitals don't   Medicare
doesn't   Three weeks is standard   The standard stay   three
weeks is   three   weeks

My Mother in the Hospital, and My Father—

                    like the cat we took in
from the cold—scarred, half blind,
quick skitter and claw—
suddenly on the counter
when my back is turned, stealing
Thanksgiving turkey, then
beneath my heel as I step from the stove.
Warm gravy splatters the floor, my clothes.

I want to scream.
I want to put him out, or lock him in an upstairs room.

And yet
he cannot help what he does
not understand.

I scratch his broken ears, stroke his spine.

I am afraid

of how hard it grows to forgive

his wiry hiss,
his purr
as he fattens on all I have dropped.

This Stage

Look at you, old
man—distant
dear crusty old
man—you, who never knew
me well, whom I
do not know,
though you are the only man I've known for all
my life. Here you are, your fever heat
beside me in the doctor's waiting room.
I take your crooked hand.
You let your eyes fall closed.
Without your bustle, your brocade of talk
on antique chests and etymologies and cans
you collected from the side of the road, without the light
of your eyes, I see
the hollows of your skull.
You, who never speak to me of age, or death, or love—
you know, don't you,
that this is how it may go—this loss
of appetite, the pull
of sleep, the days folded into pale blue
sheets. Today
we sit side by side. We act
as though you have only
a cold.
But the curtain's been pulled wide—
if not for the last act,
then for rehearsal.

I Call My Mother

Her talk floats, changes course
like blown soap bubbles. Then—

her voice gone. Someone else's
laughter comes near,

draws hers. She drifts
toward whoever

is taking her pulse,
lifting her spoon.

She does not hear me
calling

into the receiver, trying
to say goodbye.

I stand in my kitchen,
phone to my ear,

listening
to the room she is in.

Direction

They call it Speech Therapy, but they mean
    your memories   plans   the tickle of thought
        on the tip of your tongue
And
    calendars   hours
      shopping lists
        birthday gifts
Therefore,
    Can you name three foods that begin with B?
      What time does the clock say?
      What does a duck say?
And furthermore,
    How many minutes in half an hour?
      What shape is a book? A ball? A pie?
        Please read five words from the left side of this page.
        (No honey. That's not the left.
         Look   over here)

They call it Speech Therapy, but they mean
    your tongue   your lips   your throat
      your   breath
So:
    Small bites now, keep chewing
      And, *Tuck your chin first, then swallow*
        And always:
            Are you pocketing food in your cheeks?
            Use your tongue—feel the inside of your mouth.
            You could choke. You don't want to choke.
            Focus now: Chin down. Swallow. Don't choke.

They call it Speech Therapy, but they mean
    Wednesday morning
        (Really? But it's dark out)
        and Wednesday night
            (See, your reasoning skills have improved!)
They mean Thursday afternoon
   (What meal are you waiting for?)
        and your friend, coming for dinner.
          (Remember: Swallow first. Then
            talk.)

They mean hazy sun and glint of water. The names
    of the birds overhead.
        A slow-moving barge, steering you through
           the fog.

Unfiltered Light

In the sunlit exercise room, my mother sits
beside a balding, bearded man in a motorcycle jacket
to practice clipping clothespins to a paper cup.
Across the square table, a rapidly-blinking teen
and a woman with deep wrinkles
and purple hair.
They work in heavy silence.

The therapist encourages them
to use just one hand. *Don't forget,*
this is healing not just your body,
but your brain.

She passes out putty, demonstrates
how to gather it into a ball, then flatten it
with only the fingers.
Motorcycle man keeps dropping his putty.
The blinking boy breathes heavily.
The purple-haired woman bites her lip, slows,
revives when the daughter sitting behind her
pats a shoulder, whispers in her ear.

My father holds my mother's right hand
to keep her from using it.
His eyes won't stay open. His body sags sideways.
My mother tells him it's time for his nap,
looks for his hat.
Before he can step away, she reaches up
from her wheelchair to tug at his scarf. *Come here, You.*
Don't go without a proper goodbye.
They kiss.
Light touches the whole table.
Everyone blinks
as my father straightens

and my mother beams
and my father smiles
and my mother teases, *Do I know you?*
I sure hope so. If I don't,
I want to.

The Therapist Asks My Mother

The therapist asks my mother to remember
three words: *fish, garden, star*.

It is not obvious
to my mother
that her phone is not her call button.

It is not obvious
to my mother
that her left hand lies slack in her lap
as she tries to pull foil from her pudding cup.

The therapist asks her to pick the blue blocks
from a pile, put them into a bin.
My mother says, *This is so silly,*
then picks the green.

Two weeks in rehab, and already
she's putting on her shirt, feeding herself
with supervision, beginning
to stand.

The therapist asks, *Which weighs most,*
an apple, a strawberry, or a blueberry?
My mother asks how plump the blueberry, whether
the strawberry is wild. Wild strawberries
can be very small—but so sweet!

The therapist laughs and agrees. *And now,*
put these in order, from thick to thin: wrist, crayon, tree.
My mother remembers her dogwood tree. Wonders
if she's missed its bloom, though the window
holds banks of gray snow.

Three weeks, and they say she is ready
to leave. The nurses and therapists hug her
goodbye, say she's spunky and strong, say they're sure
she'll do well. Look how far
she has come. Remember
the beginning?
Fish. Garden. Star.

The Hospital Social Worker Is Available to Discuss Future Plans

1.

Don't worry,
on discharge your mother will be given prescriptions
for a visiting nurse, PT, OT, Speech.

They'll come to wherever your family decides
to move her.

Do you know where you'll move her?

2.

Does their house have an accessible entrance?
A downstairs shower?
A stair lift?
Are the doorways wide enough for her wheelchair?

Have you met with any contractors?

Has anyone spoken to you about assisted living?

3.

don't cry

even if
the home were suitable, in cases like hers—

we wouldn't advise

impulsive
a blindness to her own
the risk of

given his age, and hearing loss, your father
couldn't

not to mention
her toileting—
we don't
recommend that a spouse

unless you
were planning to

or a live-in

someone to supervise her
full-time.

Week after Week

I am the calm hand
on the elbow, the steadying
voice. The embrace.
I am the calendar. The ear on the phone.
The pen, taking notes.

I am holding my mother's dreams
to her lips.
I am wrapping my father's dread
in soft songs.

Days take the shape of
leaping.
Nights carry edges
of yet to be
done.

I feel the lines on my face
drawing tight.

I keep bruising my head
on the corners of decisions.
I am spinning.
I am swallowing my tongue.

We're So Glad Your Family Will Be Joining Our Community

1.

we'll need
for each of your parents

for our files

2.

because your father
on behalf of your mother

sign here

Part II

Unfamiliar

The way her face
seems always on the lip of a question.

The way her words have gone dull.

The way her eyes—
what is it, about her eyes?

The Glass

For weeks I've been trying to hold it steady,
to remember how full
it still is.

Now my father takes it from my hand,
tastes what's there,
then spits into the sink,
complaining of bitterness.

How Must it Be

             to be you,
and the wife you knew
would outlast you—vibrant
blue eyes, a smile you could hear
on the phone, she who knew everything
to say, to do, the glue that held home
in place—

             how must it be when she
who did not die
yet is not
her—

             how must it be when she
leans on
you
to walk these strange halls?

Sixty years. You had
your roles.
You don't know how
to be a new man,
how to hold the hours steady,
how to hold her
when she remembers,
and mourns the woman she was.

Thrown

That year, she was in the garage with her electric sander,
refinishing a second-hand table, a desk, a chair.
She was on a ladder, grouting the shower stall,
in her office, pricing old coins,
in the cellar, sorting what could stay, what should go.
That autumn, she cooked eggplant parmesan
for her husband's birthday, talked with her daughter
about planting more daffodils, tried
not to dwell on new tumors
in her son's liver,
eye, spine.

                   Now   she can't
             understand   why she   can't
         understand
     which therapists will come   which days   or how many
days she's been in this   place   how much longer
     she may have to   stay

              She sits in a   wheelchair
       at the desk brought from   home   gazing
   at bills   magazines   handwritten letters   cards

     She flips through her Rolodex
      doesn't make any   calls

          opens her planner   doesn't know
           where to place her   eyes

                 which
          week
                  which

                       month

Scattered

She tries
to sit in sunlight, but it never stays
where she left it.

Her room feels too dim.

She leans to open the blinds,
knocks over the bowl of blue marbles.

When she reaches to gather them up,
her hand knocks them farther away.

Mystery (A Question)

My mother—but not
my mother.

Her heart, her drive, her
wit, and yet—

What she says
when—

Or what she doesn't seem to—

The way her smile—
    the set of her jaw—
        the timbre of her voice—

So much sorrow.

I hold her close.

If I can name
what I miss,
will I know where to look—
how to find it in her?

From Inside Askew

From inside askew, you don't know
how you slant.

Your speech slips and circles.
Angles seem straight.

You're sure left is right,
sure we are all wrong,

don't feel yourself sliding,
don't see yourself fall.

But there you are—down on the floor,
making light of the pain in your head.

We offer our arms.
You weep, ask why.

Tilt-a-World

You were at home, knew its shadows, its bones.
You could paint it with your eyes closed,
knew it so well
that you didn't
know it after all, as one doesn't
know air.

You awoke to sun glare and daze,
the roof ripped off, walls flat on the grass.

Now you move through a stranger's rooms.

Weeks tumble by.

You keep trying
to hang your old clothes, read the clock.
The closet yawns.
The hours shrink away into gloom.

Your feet can't remember the ground.
Days taste of fog.
Your thoughts—stray cats in a field.

What Then?

Ship of bone and breath and flesh—
but what
when the mast bends like rubber,
when the rudder floats away,
when the wheel spins loose as a toy?

What
when the mind thinks *walk*
and the foot you feel moving exactly
as it used to
is, in fact, dragging—the floor rising
again
to greet your waving palms?

What
do you make of yourself then,
when the body—your own
body—ceases
to be the vessel of your intentions,
becomes, instead, your anchor?

She Can't Be Happy

She can't be happy that she now
writes tottery words in a sloping scrawl
because she can't remember
that, for weeks,
she couldn't—

only that, almost yesterday

she could jot names and numbers
while on the phone,

could list her daily to-dos,

could paint sunflowers, a porcelain vase,
a line of pears on a wooden tray,
green ripples of ribbon framing an old woman's face.

Broken Brain Blues

She's been struck by a train, now she weeps and mourns.
Struck silent but hard, how she weeps and mourns.
Whipped out of her shoes. No whistle, no horn.

Broke not a bone, but tore holes in her mind.
Days wander off through the holes in her mind.
She misses her Self. She sorrows and pines.

She's standing again, but she can't walk home.
Can't have her old shoes, can't find her way home.
No recourse. No road to where she started from.

Feels like a burden to the man in her bed.
Can't bear to burden the man in her bed.
She weeps through the night, pillow over her head.

As Though

She dreams home
into her days—
    sunlight across her desk,
    chicken thighs in her freezer,
    dogwood trees by her patio chairs.

She plans and plans
to move back,
as though, once there,
she can return to the mind
that kept order, time,
to the life where her own hands
made the meals, washed her hair,
where placing her feet before standing
was thoughtless as air.

He Stays

       by her side, leans closer
to hear her
repeat
the best route home.

Day after day, her circling
words.

How he wears thin.

He won't praise this new place,
its fluorescent chatter,
its wall-to-wall, soft-soled aides,
but he knows
what's lost,

and that, if he tells her, he'll break

her heart.

Part III

The Occupational Therapist Answers My Father

Oh, I can't make any predictions. But look—
it's only three months
since her stroke. It could be years
of improvement. It could be,
given the progress she's already
made, she'll keep right on.

She's such a joy to work with. Her humor, her warmth.
So many gains, not only physical, but emotional,
intellectual.
Look at her speech alone.
And her chewing,
her swallowing.

I can't tell you if she'll ever be okay to move home.
Not yet, for sure.
But look what she's working on now
compared to when we started.
Look how well she's been doing with a walker.
We walked the whole hall today.
Down and back.
Twice.

Meanwhile, the House

The refrigerator hums to the food in the freezer.

The beautiful useless lovelies pose on the shelves.

The windowsills collect tiny struggles—moth, ladybug, fly.

The matching bureaus ask what the dust foretells—

whether their drawers will finally be emptied, or filled.

Unsettled

There is the gap he never noticed
between leaving
and left.

He can't think
of doors never opening
again—
          all his books, shelves
in every room.

He can't bring himself to discard
their possibilities.

His chest binds when friends ask what he'll do
with the house. She
was the one
who knew how to turn a page, make sense
of fine print.

Broken Love Song

From the back of my car, my father's voice—
the first time I have ever
heard him sing:
Some of these days, you're gonna miss me.

My father—singing
a song I've never heard.
His old-man voice, off-key.
'Cause you know, honey, you had your way.

My mother, weeping—
her first trip to a store since her stroke—its high shelves,
crowded aisles. Its colors, sizes, brands, sales,
decisions.

So, from the back of the car, my father
sings my mother back
to solid ground.
An old man, off key:

And when you leave me,
you know it's gonna grieve me,
Oh, you're gonna miss
your big, fat
mamma
some of these days.

Note: The song "Some of these Days," written and composed by
Shelton Brooks, was published in 1910, and made famous by Sophie
Tucker (1886–1966)

She was happier in rehab,

        when she didn't believe
in her stroke, in spite of
her wheelchair,
her bedpan,
her idle left hand.

She spoke of the party she was planning
to host
for all the nice people
helping her bathe
and eat.

Now,
three months after
the bleed in her brain,
she quietly seethes.
She wants
a road back. Restitution.
Someone to curse. Someone
to kick in the teeth.

An Hour

She says she's ready for lunch. He puts on his shoes,
has his hands on her wheelchair
to help her downstairs, but then
she's looking for her glasses
or keys, and then
for the tote bag with spare socks,
calendar, medical records, checkbook—
the bag she likes to keep near
since she can't just pop back
to get things she might need,
and she's told him before—
she feels more secure when she has her bag
with her, so instead of his asking again
why she needs all this stuff
just to go down to lunch,
couldn't he simply do what she asks
and check in the bathroom
while she checks the desk?
Oh, and look, here's that glove
she was looking for yesterday,
could he put it on the bookshelf
by the bed? And, while he's there,
the clean sheets need to go in the closet.
And please find her blue sweater.
Or no, never mind, it's here on the chair.
She'll carry it with her to wear after lunch
when she sits outside
while he takes his walk.
Can he check today's weather?

And she's smoothing the sweater across her knees
and jingling her keys
and holding her bag and her glasses

and wanting to scream
because now he's gone back
to check the computer—now, even though
she's just told him
she's ready
for lunch.

He Can't

he can't hear
the birds   the phone   her
voice

he can't see
words in books   the nuance
of her face

he lives here   where he can't
feel at home

she is here   yet is not

her

//

it spills out
when she doesn't want him

to neaten the papers on her desk,

to remind her she's standing too far
from her walker

to help her maneuver
through the door

it spills out

it washes over his face
gets in his eyes,
his mouth
drips into his hands,
and he throws them up, fuming

      Never mind   I just can't

   do   anything

to please

you

Dream

My father's dream has a door in it.
Through the door, a silence of blue.
Blue so deep, he could wade
for miles.

For months, inside his head a garden
of pinwheels, spinning
and glaring—chaos of sun-glint and color.

For months, lists of to-do and to-be. Trying
to hold himself steady.
Trying to keep his wife
whole.

What he needs is the hush
of nobody's need.

What he needs is a cloud
with a room in it.

my mother's poem

                doesn't believe
it's a poem

it can't remember   its lines
        weeps
              apologizes

for its   blank spaces
stumbling feet
irregular
leaps
and turns—

       the burden
of its form

it wants to go back to the beginning

      it wants

to go back   to not seeing
the bottom of the page

it yearns
        for revision

the yearning lingers

in the spaces

in the silence

Valiant

Her days break
into individual tasks,
into individual portions
of tasks.
When I visit, she stops
her methodical process
of getting dressed, or washing
her hands, or sorting the mail
to tell me about the order
of her movements,
the order she's trying to impose
on her hours,
so that she'll get better,
so that she'll remember,
though she doesn't remember
that I know
what she's going to say,
that she said it already
last month,
last week,
yesterday.

Morning (This Thin-Walled Place Where She Can't Feel at Home)

She tells me she cries
in the bathroom each morning,
a towel pressed tight
to her mouth.

She has nowhere
to go
to tear out her hair,
to pound her fists
to open her lungs and
scream.

Like your grandma,

                 you've stepped off a boat
you never wanted to board,
and this shore is rocky, austere.

You pull your shawl tighter,
close your eyes,
but your family is already here,
settling in. The new life
won't let go of your bones.

Yet your thoughts keep turning
back.

Please,
look around. Find something
that draws your smile.
Like your grandma,
                 step toward it.

Proof

Four months in this place.
You think you can leave if you prove
you can do what you used to. You're eager to try
the stairs.

Your therapist reviews what you've practiced.
You turn yourself sideways, let go
of your walker, place your hands side by side on the rail.

And you climb—but not
as the therapist planned, two feet on each step, slowly, with care.
No, you go with the habit of before: foot over foot,
heels landing only on air.

The therapist grips your belt, slows you down.
We're tapping toes against risers, remember?
Don't talk. Use your eyes
to check your feet.

Four steps more, and you're talking again,
praising the food you eat here.
She draws you back. *Focus. Beware of your body*
twisting. Can you feel yourself
tilting backwards?

At the top, you are buoyant
and tired.
Eight paces away, the sitting nook, its soft armchairs.

In the space of a breath, you forget
you can't walk there alone.

The therapist springs forward, stops the fall
you do not feel coming.

Nobody Wants This Battle

So I am the one
to take my mother's arm, to walk her
again to the border, point out the new barriers,
yellow warning signs. How the ground
we once knew is now planted with mines.

But her mind veers away from belief.
She was just there, not long ago,
washing windows, raking leaves.
She is sure, if she tries hard enough,
she can live as before.

Each time I refuse
to help her cut through the barbed wire, to go
just as far as those fir trees, the brown house
in their shade, I don't know
how her gaze will shift,

how either of us
will bear
whatever comes next.

The Open Door

She refuses the aides
who come offering their hands. Instead
asks my father
to look in now and then,
just in case,
while she bathes on her own.

So good, to do it alone, however slowly.
So good, to feel that she can.

But my father stays at his desk,
barely checks on her,
and she bristles.

She doesn't see, as she once did,
that he gets through his days by avoiding
harsh light.

She doesn't feel, as she once could,
what she does to him—just asking him
to look
through that door.

Hard

Nights, she relies on him to help
if she falls while maneuvering from bed to toilet
and back
without buzzing the aides.

Days, she scolds him for hovering
when she pushes her walker too fast
down the hall.

When she stumbles
it's because he
distracted her.

When she hits him,
it's because he
isn't listening to her.

And anyway, it's been only a few times
that she's hit him.
And not even hard.

Mystery II (An Answer)

My mother is gone.
A similar sister lives
in her body.

I keep leaning closer,
toward all that she shares
with my mother.

I keep leaning closer.

I want to believe I am wrong.

But the questions
this woman doesn't
feel.
The answers
she doesn't know
how to hear.
The way this woman's face moves
over the bones and hollows of my mother's skull.

There

He knows nothing else to do.
He moves through their two rooms,
through the months,
keeping busy at his desk,
his back to her circular bustling.

But each time he returns
from his walk round the block,
she is there
on the veranda, watching the sky,
the elegant trees. Waiting
for him.

And she smiles, glad to see him again.
And he smiles, glad to see her again.
And she reaches up to touch his cheek.
And he hands her dandelions
from the side of the road.
Then he holds out his arm to help her stand,
and she pushes her walker beside him
and they go up the elevator
together
before the bickering resumes.

Part IV

Already It's Time

For months we've been putting her off, saying Wait
until spring. When you're walking better. When no one will slip
on the ice.

Now the trees are in bud. She wants to see the daffodils
she knows must be blooming in her yard.

I take her to visit.

I take her to breathe
inside her own house, to look out her own windows, to sit
on her patio

to talk
about ways to make the house safe for other visits, other days.

But she can't
stop her mind
from leaping, can't
keep her thoughts in one line.

She caroms from closet to drawer, desk to bureau,
wants me to find her stamp collection, her silver earrings,
her sketch pad and oil pastels, wants
to look at the yard-sale table waiting in the garage,
to explain how she'll fix it,
to take a quick trip to the store right now
for a slat of wood, brown paint.

And I am holding her
back, holding her steady, helping her up
the stairs she thinks she can climb alone,
helping her through hallways and doors,

reminding her to lift her left foot, to stand closer
to her walker

and six hours skitter past,

and she hasn't looked at the daffodils, has barely glanced
out the windows

and already it's time
to leave.

Her Strength

Her son is dying.
She can do nothing but sit in her wheelchair
beside his bed. His body
so gray, so thin. The tumors
so quickly
everywhere.

A few times
he wakes, looks at the faces around him
with wonder. Can't speak.

Hours.
His chest hardly rises, hardly falls.
She wants to stay with him.
She would stay for days, for as long
as it takes.

But her own gray body—it's pressures, its pulse.
Her gray husband, unsteady. Unable
to withstand   this
waiting.

So her hands have to   let go
of her son's beautiful fingers.

Her eyes have to   let go
of his face.

She lets   herself
be wheeled   away

from the last

of his breath.

Low

1.

She doesn't let herself cry
as her son's friend wheels her chair
past the nurse's station,
into the elevator,
out to the street, its rush-
hour traffic.

She weeps in the car,
aches
to turn back,
to lie down
in that white bed.

2.

She stops going
to Group Chair Exercise,
Brain Games with Beth,
Current Events.

Morning
after morning,
her whole body begs
for sleep,
begs to sink
into yawning dark.

Spirit

At the memorial service,
my mother is able to push her walker to the front
of the room, to stand before the gathered faces without falling
apart

and tell the story about making bread
with him when he was two, how she later
found dough in his diaper, in his hair, on even
the ceiling

and the story of how he gathered insects
from the yard, dragonflies and Japanese beetles
in jars. How she'd find butterfly wings fluttering
from his jeans

and the story of how he met his wife,
how each seemed to fit the empty spaces
of the other, how watching them cook was like
watching a dance

and finally the story
about the field mouse that appeared in her bathroom
the very morning her son died, how they gazed at each other
unafraid

how she imagined
her son was there, in the embrace
of those eyes, imagined he'd found his way to her, was saying
goodbye.

I'll Be the Safety Net, Stretched Taut, Waiting

She is tired of listening to people who keep saying, *No.*

She's now that girl who walks out of school
on a very bad day, not thinking
her absence will knot her parents' guts,
not thinking past the wash of her own sorrow,
wide and gray as the sea.

She is the girl leaning far out the window
of the speeding car, never doubting
the rush of air on her summer skin,
never doubting the force of her will
is enough to keep her safe.

Cardboard boxes already clutter the floor.

She beams as she speaks of returning to life
back home.

My father rests a palm on her shoulder.
They joke and tease.
She's improved so steadily.
She shines with certainty.
He believes.

//

He says he gave notice this morning.

She says not to worry, they'll handle it
all.

He says these rooms are so small,
moving out won't be hard.

She says she never buzzes the aides here, she won't
need aides there.

When I speak of the front steps, the stairway, the shower
at home, of cooking, errands, transportation, chores,
he says, *We've managed before. We'll do it again.*

She says, *You don't have to*
get involved. It's not your
burden.

//

They want capers, cumin, garlic. Fresh basil
in the salad. Blue cheese.
They want olives with the pits. The whole
chicken—skin and bone and dark.
They want the carcass
for soup. They'll risk
a few spills.

They need
to try,
to know what will happen
if they try.

//

He speaks of escaping
the bingo, the sing-alongs,
the bland faces, bland chatter.
He thinks he can see well enough
to do what she
used to,

as long as she tells him
what to do. He thinks
he can hear well enough to hear her
instructions. He doesn't think
of what a woman holding her walker
can't lift or carry or clean.
He doesn't know
how much time he would have to give
to rinsing salad greens, bringing plates to the table.
He doesn't know how often she'd want him
to wash the sheets, or how long it would take
to help put them back on the bed,
or how little of the day he'd have left
after sorting the groceries
and sweeping the floor, and keeping watch
outside her bathroom door. I know
it is hope
that carries him away.
Eight months
here. He feels buried alive
in this place full of waiting
to die.

The Leaf, as it Falls

How it catches and turns
on inflections of air.

If I measured
the force and angle of the wind,
the weight and form of the leaf,

could I see
where the day would take it?

See enough
to know
how it would fall?

Then, Somehow

Cheryl from SeniorCare
stands in the musty living room
telling me she has many
clients like my parents, who can't believe
they need help.
She tells them to think
of their loved ones, the worry.
That hiring aides is a gift
to their—
      then she asks,
Are you an only child?

I am   a fish,
my mouth opening, closing,
my eyes round
and staring.

And already she is saying
Oh! I'm sorry.   *Oh*
I'm so
sorry.

These waters have always
circled the earth.
We fall,
fall again
into sudden gray pools.
                Then,
        somehow,
the surface smooths

and we are walking
and talking again.

Turkish Fig

my hand   opening
the cabinet door   the sound
of hinges

the fig
between my fingers   between
my teeth

my mother
and father—going

my brother—gone

taste
the fading
of taste

this life   its folds
and textures

what my tongue knows

now

as opposed to

now

Help

Because he's so hard of hearing,
my father places the chair exactly
where my mother asked him
not to.

She wants him to move it aside.
He asks why she keeps changing her mind.
She tries not to cry.
He throws his hands in the air.

The aide arrives, feels
the storm hovering,

puts on the tea,
tells my father she's still laughing at that joke
he told yesterday,
rests a palm on my mother's arm,
moves the chair from the path of her walker

and shifts
the air in the room,
saving
a small square of the world.

My Mother's Gaze

Always the sun coming out
tomorrow,
always the better days
ahead

so her heart keeps waiting
for roses,
her hands never open
the book in her lap,
her thoughts leap past
this

rain, how it lifts the scent of green,
how my father leans toward her
with a folded blue handkerchief,
wipes droplets from her glasses,
from her cheeks.

Druthers

If I had my druthers, my mother likes to say.
If I had mine, my mother would know
her new self.
Most days she tries
to carry her own
coffee, her own tears. Most days
she stumbles,
doesn't fall because the aide
is there.
So she doesn't believe,
says she doesn't need
this much help. She needs
her own space.
If she had her druthers, she'd have privacy.
Then she could tend the inside of her head.
Her eyes would focus on the novels she wanted to read.
Her ears would hold on to the evening news.
She'd remember
the day of the week, the hour
of my visit. She'd take back
her calendar, give me
all the years she waited too long to give herself.
She would give her life for me.

Walking the Dog in the Cold, I Wonder about the First Hats

I imagine animal
skins, the necessity
of putting all offerings of hard lives
to good use.

I wonder
at the thought of someone carving a needle
out of bone,
of someone thinking to draw sinew
through needle's eye,
draw needle through hide
that someone found a way to clean, to make dry
and pliable, to shape
for the curves of human
lives.

I wonder
how we keep coming up with answers
to weather we can't bear.

Today, the first winter
afterwards,
I took out the knit hat
you once sent for my birthday.

I took it out
and put it on
and felt

better.

Taking This In

(In the first spring of the Covid-19 pandemic)

My mother sits in her kitchen while I stand
on her patio, our palms pressed
to the sliding glass door
as we speak on our phones.

She must have misplaced her glasses today. I notice
the shape of her cheekbones, how much warmth
in her eyes. She beams
as she did in the hospital, those first dreamy weeks
after her stroke, before
she understood.
Today she is radiant, more radiant than I have seen her
in over a year. Today she is the most beautiful
woman I have ever seen.

We do not go near what hovers around us—the lesson
floating on the air we don't dare to share.
I don't know when or whether
I'll ever touch her again.
But right now, if she has considered
how long these strange days may go on,
she isn't dwelling on it. She is smiling. We can't seem to stop
smiling.

I remember how brightly she laughed when she first tried
to stand after her stroke *(My legs fell asleep!)*
I remember her ease with the nurse who held her
in front of the commode *(We're slow dancing!)*
while a second nurse cleaned her behind.

Now she says, as she says every day when I call,
that she hasn't done anything
useful—but today

96

she's decided it's okay, she is lucky
to have help, she's letting herself be happy
to be queen for a while.
I draw a heart on the glass, kiss it.
She grasps her walker, pushes to stand, kisses back.

When my father comes into the room, she hands him
the phone, asks him to explain
what she's been struggling to arrange
into words—the history they learned
on that documentary yesterday.
Wonder and pleasure move over her face
at the ease of his language—ancient Egypt, pharaohs
and deities—but I am not really listening
because she is leaning her head against his body
as he stands behind her chair, and he
is resting his palm on her arm,
and I watch her drifting
on the rise and fall of his voice. I watch her
gazing out at the sky, at the trees, at me.
She finds my eyes, mouths, *I love you,*

and I am still
standing outside the glass door, taking all of this in.

About the Author

Jennifer L Freed's poetry appears in various print and on-line journals including *America, Atlanta Review, Atticus Review, Connecticut River Review, The Worcester Review,* and *Zone 3,* as well as in various anthologies, such as *Forgotten Women, a Tribute in Poetry* (Grayson Books, 2017); *Aftermath: Explorations of Loss and Grief* (Radix Media, 2018); *Feminine Rising* (Cynren Press, 2019), and others. Her chapbook, *These Hands Still Holding* (Finishing Line), was a finalist for the 2013 New Women's Voices contest. She is the recipient of the 2020 Samuel Washington Allen Prize for a long poem or a poem-sequence, and her poetry has been nominated for a Pushcart Prize. She lives in central Massachusetts.

Jfreed.weebly.com